The Chronicles

of the

Wandering Man

Michael E Bell

Winner of the Fanstory.com Seal of Quality award

Produced with Amazon Kindle Direct
Publishing (KDP)

First Published, 2012

Michael Bell

Michael E Bell

Chapter 1:

Mother Dust

I

A few breaths past forever's night,
with Dawn a strangled memory,
I choke upon the afterlife
of xenophobic fury.

The dust cakes lungs and soils my air
with evil's dark excreta,
my life become thick boles of dung
Hate riddled with his cancer.

I look across an Earth bleached grey
by atoms' tortured pleas;
a paranoid metropolis,
an empty legacy.

With horror's black yet verdant hope
I quest 'cross landscapes raped,
a tiny ant with solace dreams -
from this world to escape.

II

A hundred years or so ago,
the blight tore through this land
with fetid breath and acid bile
and dealings underhand.

No dog of war was our demise,
no politics our loss.
It was the deals, grotesque and grim,
the winning against cost.

As lust became our currency
and testing was a virtue,
poor Mother Nature bled upon
the beds of profit's nurture.

Eventually, the land was dry,
no creature found a mate.
The world, in all its innocence,
fell victim to our hate.

III

Now radiation suckles me
upon a nuclear teat.
The fallout fuels my apathy
and no day is discrete.

Although I breathe, I live in death –
a zombie all alone,
as though the devil drinks my breath
and soaks my very bones.

What animal have I become,
existing just to stroll,
inhabiting this purgatory
with no hope of parole?

I only know that I must seek
a purpose where I can.
Through desolation's aftermath,
I am the Wandering Man.

Chapter 2:

The Cuckoo and the Eldritch Kiss

IV

A Cuckoo called my name tonight
and broke my pointless sleep.
It dragged me from my nightmare's hold
and suicide's cold creep.

I shook the shadows from my head
and gathered up my world;
a rucksack, packed with who I am,
my dull brown flag unfurled.

That bird-call was a prophecy,
a warning to beware
that Death was out there, stalking me,
and fixed me with his stare.

I shouldered hope and scored the land
as, heading dark to dark,
I sought the source of nature's caw,
my guardian angel lark.

V

I came upon a place of home;
a building that still stood,
with droopy door and sleepy windows'
memories of wood.

The Cuckoo's call had led me here
in deference to my quest,
but night yet tried to hide from me
the jewel it could divest.

Eventually I found my boon,
my sustenance of food
in tins sealed tight against the smog
of fallout's rancid brood.

As fibre filled my womb with hope,
determination's fuel
was spice upon this rarest meal.
Starvation's madness cooled.

VI

The bedroom spawned a precious tear,
a fresh line on my cheek.
Two skeletons hugged on a bed
decayed, macabre and meek.

Their eldritch mouths touched in a kiss,
a love defying death.
I wept in honour of their lives,
remembering lovesick breaths.

I covered up their modesty
with moth-worn blanket's cloud
and searched their sanctuary for aid;
I never felt less proud.

I came upon a gun and shells,
still oiled and well preserved;
security and danger mixed,
a cold comfort absurd.

VII

I hit my path with vim renewed
and strode into the void
of shadows clutching at the earth,
no longer paranoid.

I knew that I must find a place
of haven in this land,
and so I wandered, determined,
across the hostile sand.

I chanced upon a rocky crag
and narrow valley's mouth.
My instincts set ablaze my mind
with dark warnings uncouth.

I grabbed my pistol from my waist
and primed a ready shot,
but then a cold click rang behind:
This might just be my lot.

Chapter 3:

The Treacherous Tree

VIII

The coffin's click assailed my ears,
my heartbeat drummed out notes.
Thoughts flooded with a treacle sea,
but Fear - the bastard - floats.

A woman, leather-bound and dark,
her eyes gun barrel ends,
had pinned my careless self against
a rock with rifle's lens.

I saw her tendons tighten 'gainst
the trigger's hairline clasp
and threw myself into a roll
to her frustrated gasp.

"I seek not death!" I yelled aloud,
and threw my gun aside.
This filthy, deadly, rarest girl
could not in hate reside.

IX

Her gun on me, she told me of
communities survived,
of how they eked a hellish life,
existence never thrived.

With panic in her desperate gaze,
she bade me move along
before the others saw me as
a brick to make them strong.

"You cannot understand," she said,
"this isn't what you need,"
but I would sacrifice all time
for ten minutes of creed.

Reluctantly, she took me down
into the valley's maw.
Despite her pessimistic tone,
this was my dream restored.

X

Within an hour, the night played host
to kidnap's treachery,
as ambushers cloaked in the dark
had strapped me to a tree.

She'd looked at me with silent eyes,
a mute testimony
to how a lonely heart is tricked
by thoughts of company.

The rock-dead wood pressed at my back
like nature's cold revenge.
My captors jigged and chanted like
demons in their demesne.

Their gazes fed upon my form
with fever's fervoured lust.
Three men insane. One frightened girl.
Me and my foolish trust.

Chapter 4:

Black Moon Glinting

XI

The dull illumination's pall
sent shadow 'cross the scene.
The sun, these days behind the smog;
Black Moon, dead light obscene.

My captors chanted, sang and jerked,
and brandished shivs and sticks
as though the Radiation's stage
cast them as lunatics.

I knew the fate that robbed their minds
and kept my body young
while every human molecule
was by its hangman strung.

Despite their vicious, sick intent,
I didn't own the blame
to hate these creatures, pitiful.
All victims. All the same.

XII

They kicked up nature's detritus
and moved in for the kill
while at the back my captor girl
stood wide-eyed, frozen still.

Medusa; Gorgon, my demise,
now petrified by fear.
Her snakes my desperation,
my crime a single tear.

As cunning violence rent the air
and blades strove for my blood,
she came to life and hefted arms,
a serpent in the mud.

My plundered gun her shining sword,
she set their demons free.
Their thoughts became but crimson clouds;
their dreams rained over me.

XIII

She loosed my bonds and begged me to
forgive her cruel deceit;
with food so rare in this black glare,
I was a source of meat.

My liberated captors draped
across the sticky ground;
my first taste of community
in decades never found.

I told her I could understand
the fear that drove her wrong;
dead people in a dying land
have nowt to keep them strong.

She took my hand and sparks aroused
determination's cue.
We'd join our strengths, resume the hunt
for life regained anew.

XIV

We watched eternal starless night
as if to seek a way,
and then that moon winked down at us,
black glinting light at play.

The birth of possibilities
then burgeoned in my mind.
If sun could flash, the world could heal;
regenesis defined.

Our memories didn't hold our names
or stale identity,
but in this barren, hopeless world,
I now had hope for me.

Night Adam in a lifeless waste,
Night Eve to plant a tree.
The future would be ours to mould;
perhaps my destiny?

Chapter 5:

Interlude - What Came Before

(i)

Mutations soaked the air, that night,
and drowned the world in dark;
a wave of chemical demise
that left the blackest mark.

The reaper was a scientist,
apocalypse foretold
by meddling with such fragile cloth;
the fabric of the world.

He rode a steed of good intent
upon a path of hope,
but paved inferno's flaming road;
the final misanthrope.

His name consigned to dust's lament,
his legacy is death;
existence now reformed in dirt
and Lonesome's shallow breath.

(ii)

I clawed my way from underground,
a rubble cradle's clutch.
I heaved a gulp of Poison's air
with lungs coated in smutch.

The burrows of the deepest trains
had kept me in their clasp,
as though the day had 'come a sword,
the night my hasp to grasp.

I knew I was a man, those days,
a person on the Earth,
my name forgotten out of need,
my past a blank since birth.

I wandered from life's wreckage with
a will to walk away
from history and memories past;
society's dismay.

(iii)

I walked for weeks before the pang
of hunger halted me,
the air alive with nourishment;
extended destiny.

I knew my natural life had gone,
replaced with acid's fee,
but even then I didn't know
I'd walk through centuries.

Eventually, I understood;
the world was down to me,
and Atlas handed me his weight's
responsibility.

I set out to discover him;
the man who signed our writ.
The world needed a target's face
to drag it from the pit.

Chapter 6:

In Flick'ring Light, Bells Toll

XV

We strode into the dawn's soft dark
with light held twixt our palms,
intentions mapping Destiny
but Fate penning our psalms.

The lonely land was welcoming
to our intruders' gait.
Each footstep both a scorpion's kiss
and petty balm too late.

Yet willing wind whipped up a wake,
our progress tracked in dust.
The world, despite our race's hate,
was welcoming of us.

We walked, a couple meek and small,
and sought our final goal,
no longer aimless or alone.
I willed my world to stroll.

XVI

The acres passed beneath our feet
and acorns turned to trees.
The years drove sun to shyly peep
through black sky's storm-swept seas.

We ate of our companionship;
a feast served up by love,
two bottom-feeding shadow crabs
become a soaring dove.

As we evolved to suckle hope
and learn again to breathe
without the poison's nurturing,
the daytime sought reprieve.

We came to know a happiness,
a freedom of a sort,
in us a perfect symmetry
not to our past distort.

XVII

But beauty cannot have her way
while evil draws a breath,
and dirty Fate came out to play
just as we cheated death.

Despite the decade spent as two,
we knew work still remained.
We still sought to the world renew;
repentance for the stains.

As prophecy dogged at our heels
uneasy and afraid,
we felt the toll of doleful bells
through air now tasting staid.

Somewhere ahead, humanity
had dug itself a hole,
and t'ward the peals of travesty
we wandered with our souls.

Chapter 7:
The Wishing Well of Fate

XVIII

We found the town that fateful day,
that hateful, fatal place
replete with greetings' violent smile;
a gun trained on my face.

The eyes behind were wild with hyp
that bred with unhinged zeal,
their gaze a hungry, feral greed,
our sanity their meal.

The town was decked in Devil's garb
and beauty come to harm.
Black bells rang out at every hour;
a call to prayer and arms.

The air was choked with grease and fear
while malice walked the streets.
All peace had left this loveless place
to fester in deceit.

XIX

They herded us by gun and boot
into a rotting shed,
ostensibly for quarantine
against infection's spread.

We knew we had to find a way
to help the light return,
and from this fetid, dirty place
the madness must all burn.

Eventually they kicked us, bound
and gagged, to face a judge.
They sat us by the village well
to sate a spiteful grudge.

Our freedom was a symbol of
the life they had denied,
and justice had no guiding hand
in what they might decide.

XX

An oil pump hammered up and down
to give this town its life,
and from its shadow crawled the judge
to underline our strife.

Decayed, decrepit, rotting eyes
with madness housed within
alighted on our hog-trussed forms
with vile and proud chagrin.

"You are accursed, you evil fiends!"
the judge yelled to the sky.
"Only the Lord can save your souls,
you cannot him deny."

With that he ordered guns to bear
upon our helpless forms.
I leaned against my bride of night
and waited for the storm.

XXI

No saviour, I, to help this place,
messiah to the world.
Instead my quest was just my pride
around my dead heart curled.

The love I found was all for naught,
I saw as powder bloomed.
The future world would bow to this;
the evil that men do.

And then Dark Eve became a cloak
thrown bloody over me,
her body flung to save my life
and possibilities.

To yells of hate and anguished tears,
I hurled myself away
into the wishing well of Fate,
and as I fell, I prayed.

Chapter 8:

Interlude - A Prayer and a Sermon

The Wandering Man's Prayer

i

I never understood the faith
that drove the flock to you,
nor could condone the hapless fate
you left them in to stew.

I see apostles up above,
all victims of your crime,
adrift upon insanity
you built in your design.

They think they do your work, oh God,
by culling freedom's peace.
They think their hate won't count when
comes
your final armistice.

Instead of helping heal the world,
you leave these monsters free,
and now I know you won't save them.
You leave that up to me.

ii

I see in you a callous god,
a petty deity,
and now I have faith, finally,
that you will fail to see

the ramollescence this world needs
to rise from horror's seethe;
the freedom I must gift to it,
the air it craves to breathe.

My partner was my link to hope
but now I wear her life.
I have a stomach full of grief
where once I had a wife.

And so I pray to you, my Lord,
who dwells in ethers fey.
I pray you'll see the only course,
and stay out of my way.

The Judge's Sermon

i

The day the holy mushroom cloud
delivered us from sin,
He gave to us, the strong and proud,
the tools we need to win.

Beneath the purity of night,
for decades we have lived
to bring us to our time of might,
to live and thrive herewith.

This frontier town has been our ark
to shield us from The End.
Now we'll maintain this perfect dark
until his will amend.

I am the prophet, sent by God
to spread his holy voice,
the shepherd sent to steer you from
freedom's anarchic vice.

ii

So follow me, ye ragged few,
into the future's care,
and understand we live our lives
beneath his blessed stare.

No traitor's words will stay our hand,
no lies will hold us down.
No shadow fiend can understand
our burgeoning renown.

We are the world, these coming times!
We are the sacred might!
We are the chosen children of
the Lord's eternal night!

We are the children: SHOUT FOR ME!
We are theandric dark!
And in our midnight, cast from earth,
the world will bear our mark!

Chapter 9:

From Black Depths, Light Abounds

XXII

The Earth's intestines clutched my form
with muck and grimy mire,
a depth of horror past forlorn
to stoke my anger's fire.

I'd landed in the blackest slime,
soaked in the town's dark blood;
a buried abattoir of filth,
a lake of oil and mud.

The pump was groaning up above,
the ground growled of its loss.
The air was shuddering with fear
as man stole Earth's black gloss.

I knew, then, Mother wanted help
and I could be her knight.
This lake - the folly of their greed -
could undo numbers' might.

XXIII

I rummaged through my carry-sack
with need fuelling my stare
until I found combustion's birth
adorned within a flare.

With grim design and grimmer face,
I clambered through the dark
and climbed foundations of the pump
without a sound to hark.

In desperate times we find a way
to dig up what is right
from ages-buried treasure troves
we choked with our insight.

Into dry dusk I made my way,
a creature of the deep,
clad thick in murk and cold lament
for crops I must now reap.

XXIV

I trudged unto the village well
and sank to weary knees.
I bellowed out a primal yell
for all the flock to heed.

They came to me with angered awe
across collective face -
they saw my mercy like a rock;
the fate they must embrace.

The Judge approached to spell my death
with but a violent point,
but then my flare lit up the night.
"The darkness I anoint!"

I watched their faces bow to fear
as light slipped down the well,
these misled fools I'd not allow
to sound the Earth's death knell.

XXV

The fire burned out the world that day
and gorged on holy air.
It supped on lives brought up on lies
and stripped the dead land bare.

The sky lit up with flaming light -
a visit from the sun -
the long-black air lit up as bright
as powder from a gun.

The town was taken by the clouds,
become but motes of dust.
The Judge, his hate, his every heir
I gave to higher trust.

I cannot know if 'Arbiter'
was my job to assume.
I only know this crater's depth
will be my sad heirloom.

Chapter 10:

Terra Sanctum,

A Shadow on the Grey

XXVI

Now picture this: a requiem,
the black upon the grey.
A world insane from lack of light
and decades' dark dismay.

The sun long hid, in fervour lost
to violent children's play.
The shadowless and bone-chill cold,
the black chagrin display.

In fear, we played ambition's game
and gave our light away
to humbly set our knees to earth
and join with midnight's fray.

With craven lust for power's trust,
quintessence of our hate,
we killed our Terra Sanctum home.
Redemption comes too late.

XXVII

Ash; acrid black, a bitter taste
to wake the screaming pain,
each breath a hacking agony
to wheeze of my refrain.

Each blistered sore a flaming eye
to strip away my thoughts
and gaze upon the guilty depths
to which I dared resort.

My shattered form was animate
and muscles clung to bone,
but skin was now a blackened crisp
and burnt flesh my cologne.

The town was gone by fire and air;
a kiss blown to the sky,
black liquid burst into a bloom
to teach the dead to fly.

XXVIII

A few blinks past revenge's flames,
once more I walked alone,
my body healed by mutant genes,
my bandages cursed bones.

Grey sky now pulsed in daily time
and soon I'd see the light.
No longer were all days denied
defining noon and night.

The world, at peace without the noise
of torrid human life,
was finding health despite the hand
with which we fed it strife.

The cycle turned by bird and tree
would bear the future's get,
without bipedal interference,
each day dusk would set.

XXIX

My shadow cooled a salad shoot
thrust bravely at the clouds;
triumphant photosynthesis
had birthed despite the shroud.

I hadn't seen the shadow man
for decades; ten or more,
and in his dark I saw the light
tired Mother had in store.

The world was perfect without us.
The beauty of her form
had led me to man's final breath
to quell all chance of storm.

As dawn burst through the ashen wall
to light the first new day,
I chose a gravestone for mankind,
an outline 'gainst the grey.

XXX

Strange fruit upon a rancid tree;
a gallows grown from guilt.
A silhouette in life's expanse,
bereft of what we built.

Strange fruit upon a rancid tree
to feed the future's gain,
a rotting, flapping epitaph,
one final eldritch stain.

Strange fruit upon a rancid tree,
the end of all we made
by pillage, rape, and plunder's boot
and pride's poor serenade.

Strange fruit upon a rancid tree
so God will understand:

In desolation's aftermath,

I am the hanging man.

Glossary

Definitions for the more obscure words used:

Demesne - pronounced 'Dee-Men', meaning 'a man's domain, land, or holdings'
Smutch - to blacken with or blackened by soot
Hyp - a morbid depression
Ramollescence - a softening or mollifying
Theandric - created / inspired by God or the divine

Technical Specification

For those who are interested ...

Your format was quatrains, grouped by fours
into thirty seven parts

Your rhyme scheme was ABCB, with some
partial rhyme thrown into the mix

Your meter was alternating lines of iambic
tetrameter and trimeter, with occasional
additional feminine end syllables

Your word count was 3,354

ABOUT THE AUTHOR

Michael E Bell was born in 1976 on planet Earth, and usually he likes to live there. He cut his teeth on poetry at the tender age of eight, and spent his school years looking for the narratives behind lesson plans.

Now, he spends his days keeping up with all the stories backed up in his head, trying to write them before they defect in search of a less barmy outlet. Sometimes, you see, the words want to play, and woe betide he who ignores them.

Want to Know More?

If you'd like to be informed of new releases by Michael E Bell and news about upcoming adventures, please check out the Michael E Bell facebook page:

https://www.facebook.com/authormichaelebell

www.ingramcontent.com/pod-product-compliance
Lightning Source LLC
Chambersburg PA
CBHW020607030426
42337CB00013B/1257